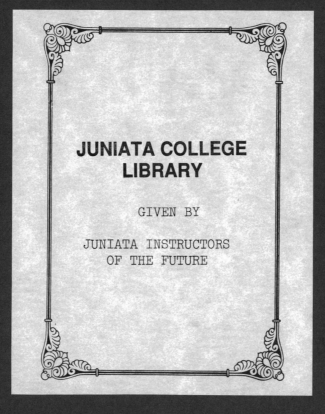

What Food Is This ?

Rosmarie Hausherr

 SCHOLASTIC INC.　New York

The foods we eat which give us strength, health, and joy, are given to us from living plants and animals. By treating our earth's resources with respect, we can show our gratitude for nature's generosity.

R. H.

Acknowledgments

I would like to thank the many people who helped with this book:
The children who were photographed at my studio or on location, and their patient parents. The friends in Vermont who let me roam in their gardens and on their farms in search of the perfect vegetable, fruit, or animal. A big thank-you to Marilyn and David Magnus who were my supportive hosts for an entire summer while I worked on this book. I am also grateful to the Kempton family; the Labree family; Felix Wey; Switzerland; Paul Clemons, who shared his secret chanterelle patch; and the Bognars, whose espressi perked up the writing.

I am thankful for the support of the Peacham Library, VT; the Johnny Appleseed's Farm, Ellington, CT; The University of Vermont Extension Service, St. Johnsbury, VT; Twin Spruce Apiaries, Climax, NY; The California Artichoke Advisory Board; The Third Street Music School, NY; Corlears School, NY; Balducci's, NY; Mr. and Mrs. Gehman, AGWAY, Manheim, PA; and New York City Greenmarkets, Barry Benepe, director, and his resourceful staff.

I appreciate the professional expertise from David Magnus, Science Teacher; Nellie Loo, MD, Department of Community Medicine, St. Vincent's Hospital, NY; Elisabeth Luder, Ph.D., assistant professor of pediatrics, Mount Sinai School of Medicine, NY; Kathy Backer, New England Dairy and Food Council, South Burlington, VT.

I am grateful to my editor, Dianne Hess, an advocate for healthful foods, who guided me through the nutritional and botanical mazes. And to the art director, Claire Counihan, an enthusiastic gourmet cook. My thanks also go to Inge Druckrey, the designer, who created another handsome book. And to Anthony Kramer whose line drawings add a fine touch.

Words that are in *italic* in the text are explained in the glossary on page 37.

Library of Congress Cataloging-in-Publication Data
Hausherr, Rosmarie.   What food is this? / Rosmarie Hausherr.
p.   cm.
Summary: Discusses, in question-and-answer format, eighteen different foods representing the four food groups and provides additional information on nutrition, healthy eating habits, and meal preparation with kids in mind.
ISBN 0-590-46583-X
1. Food—Juvenile literature.   [1. Food. 2. Questions and answers.]   I. Title.
TX355.H419   1994   641.3—dc20   93-17328   CIP   AC

12   11   10   9   8   7   6   5   4   3   2   1   3   4   5   6   7   8/9
Printed in the U.S.A.   37
First Scholastic printing, March 1994

 What food comes from grass
that an animal has eaten?

Dairy

Grass-eating cows and goats produce MILK to feed their young. The *roughage* from grass and hay is digested in four different stomachs and turned into milk.

Every morning and evening, at the same times, the herd returns to the stable. The dairy animal munches grain, while the farmer cleans the *udder* and milks by hand or machine. The warm, foaming milk is cooled and trucked to the *dairy*. There it is *pasteurized*, *homogenized*, and shipped to stores, or it is made into fresh butter, cheese, yogurt, or ice cream.

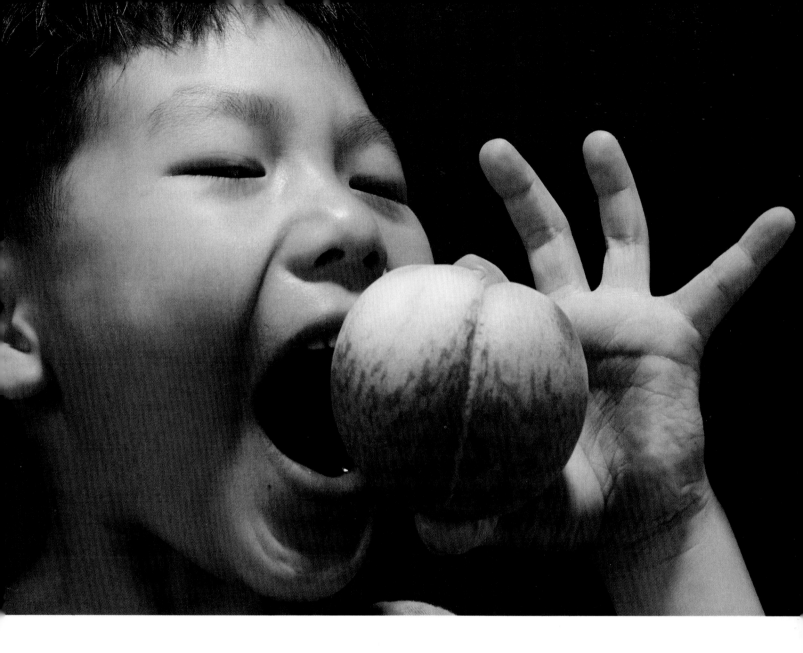

 What food wears a fuzzy coat?

Fruits/Vegetables

PEACHES, like many other fruits, grow on trees in gardens and in orchards. In early spring, the fruit trees burst into bloom. Bees gather *pollen* from their blossoms for honey and pollinate other flowers. From the center of each flower, a tiny green fruit develops. *Nourished* by sun and rain, the fruit ripens, is picked, and is shipped to stores.

Inside each peach is a large stone-like seed. Plant the seed, and another tree will grow. The fragrant ripe fruit can be squeezed into refreshing juice or dried for a sweet snack.

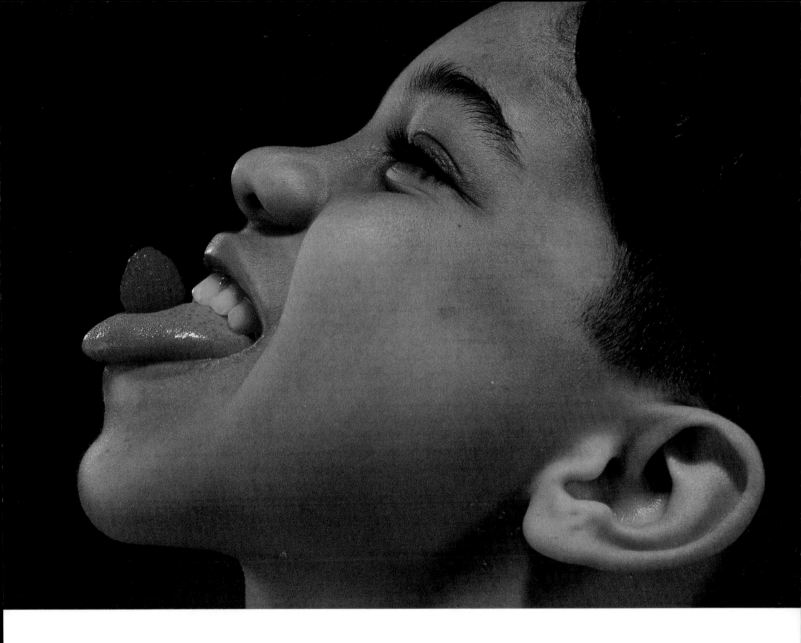

 What sweet food grows on a thorny bush?

Fruits/ Vegetables

RASPBERRIES belong to the rose family. They grow on thorny bushes in gardens or in the wild. These native fruits develop from small white blossoms that turn into sour green berries. By midsummer they are ripe, red, and sweet. They are called *aggregates* because each berry is a cluster of tiny fruits with seeds.

Picking wild berries, like blackberries, gooseberries, or blueberries, is worth a few scratches or insect bites. Wild berries taste best sun-ripened from the bush. But they also make great pies, jams, jellies, and flavorful juices.

 What foods are flowers that we eat?

CHIVE FLOWERS

ASPARAGUS FLOWERS

ARTICHOKE FLOWER

BROCCOLI FLOWERS

Fruits/Vegetables

The BROCCOLI and CAULIFLOWER we eat are flowers of the broccoli and cauliflower plants. They belong to the cabbage family. We eat their flower buds before they bloom. The bud of the ARTICHOKE is another tasty flower. If not harvested, this thistle plant bursts into a gigantic, purple blossom.

Most green plants eventually flower. But most flowers are not edible. We eat the asparagus *stalk*, but not its tiny bell-shaped flowers. We cook the bulbs of onions, chives, and garlic, but we don't eat their pretty flowers.

What food grows without seeing the sun?

Fruits/Vegetables

The crunchy orange CARROT is a *root* vegetable that grows from a tiny *seed*. The carrot plant's lacy green leaves manufacture more food from the sun than the plant needs to live. So the extra food moves down to the underground root. Because of this, carrots, beets, turnips, radishes, and parsnips are very nutritious foods. Root vegetables can be stored for winter in a dark, moist place.

Potatoes, yams, and peanuts also grow underground. One plant can produce a small *crop*.

 What food looks like a miniature cabbage?

Fruits/ Vegetables

BRUSSELS SPROUTS belong to the cabbage family. A long time ago, cabbage plants were scrawny wild cabbage weeds. Over the centuries, Brussels sprouts, kale, collards, broccoli, and cauliflower were developed from these wild weeds into big, healthy vegetables. Today's small Brussels sprout rosettes survive in cold weather, and can be harvested in the snow.

Among the large group of vegetables whose green leaves we eat are chard, spinach, and lettuce. *Chlorophyll* and sun make them green.

 What foods are called vegetables but are really fruits?

Fruits/Vegetables

Because CUCUMBERS, EGGPLANTS, PEPPERS, TOMATOES, SQUASH, PEAS, BEANS, and PUMPKINS are not sweet, we call them vegetables. But they are really fruits. The part of a plant that has seeds in it is always the fruit. Any other part—the leaves, the root, or the stalk—is the vegetable.

The next time you eat any of these colorful, vine-ripened foods in salads, casseroles, pasta sauces, or as your favorite dinner vegetable, remember you are eating fruit!

 What food tastes great when cooked on an open fire?

Proteins

Steak, hamburger, chicken, or sausage, MEATS sizzling over charcoal fires are outdoor barbecue favorites.

Our meats come from livestock, which are living animals. Cows, pigs, lambs, and chickens live on farms where they are raised on grass, grains, hay, or whey. When they grow big enough, they are brought to a slaughterhouse and killed. The butcher cleans and cuts the meat. Then it is delivered to stores.

People called vegetarians do not eat meat for spiritual or health reasons.

 What food swims in water?

Proteins

Freshwater FISH live in lakes and streams. Saltwater fish share their ocean homes with many other sea creatures, like shrimp, lobsters, squid, and mussels.

Fish are *cold-blooded* animals covered with shiny scales. Breathing through *gills*, they feed underwater on *plankton*, insects, or small fish.

Fish are caught with lines or nets. Before cooking, they are cleaned, and the scales are scraped off. Often the bones are removed. Fish are sold fresh, frozen, canned, dried, or smoked.

 What food looks like colored gravel?

Proteins

Native Americans harvested colorful peas and beans, or LEGUMES, before Columbus arrived.

Delicate pea and bean flowers on climbing *vines* mature into fruit. Peas and beans grow in pocket-like *pods*, which are shells for the plants' seeds. Removed from their pods and dried, legumes can keep for years. Protein-rich legumes are favorite meat substitutes for vegetarians. The wide variety includes chick-peas, lentils, soybeans, and peanuts — which are not nuts, but peas!

 What food is packed in a fragile shell?

Proteins

EGGS are laid by chickens on farms or in fenced-in yards.

Like wild birds, hens lay eggs in nests to hatch young chicks. Because farmers remove the eggs for people to eat, hens keep laying more. Chicken eggs are white or brown. Small greenish eggs come from pheasants. Big white ones are laid by geese, and speckled eggs come from wild turkeys.

Protein-rich eggs are a favorite breakfast food. Used for baking, they color a cake with a rich, natural yellow.

 What food is a seed hiding in a hard shell?

Proteins

Imagine a tree as high as a six-story house. The enormous
WALNUT tree grows from a small seed. The seed is the walnut
that we enjoy in desserts or just by itself. When it is pressed
into oil, it is used on salads and for cooking.

On the tree, the growing walnut is covered with a green
husk. The husk turns brown and cracks open when the nut
inside is ripe. Like pecans, hazelnuts, and almonds, the walnuts'
shells are hard and must be broken with a nutcracker.

Beautiful furniture is made from the tree's valuable wood.

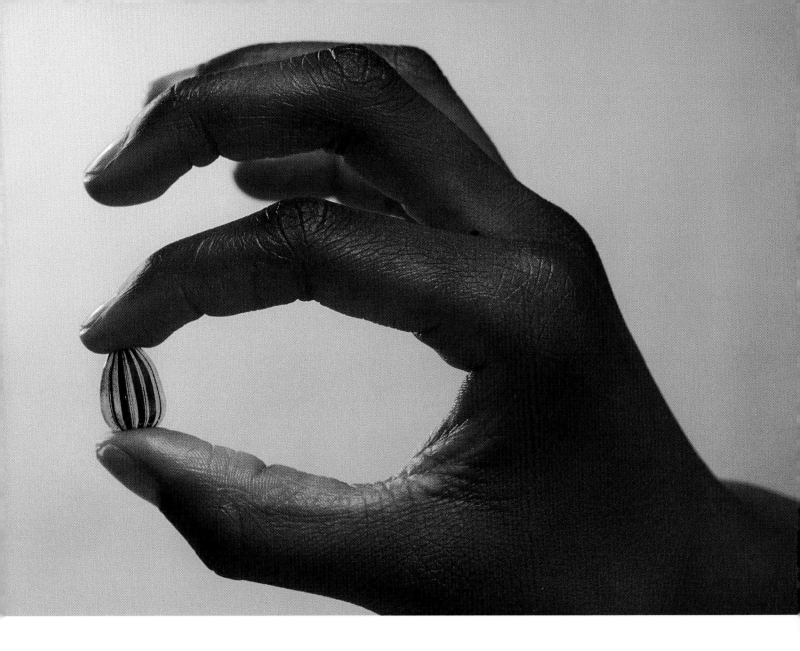

 What food comes from a pretty flower?

Proteins

SUNFLOWER SEEDS are a gift from the lovely sunflower plant.

By midsummer the plant stands as tall as a basketball player. Sunny bright-yellow petals invite bees to collect pollen from hundreds of tiny blossoms crowded together in the center of the flower. By summer's end the blossoms are dry and are pushed off by the ripening seeds. Birds feast on these seeds. Those seeds that drop to the ground may grow into flowers next year.

People enjoy sunflower seeds raw or roasted. A quality oil is made from pressed seeds.

 What foods are grass seeds?

BARLEY

RYE

WHEAT

OAT

Grains

Wild grass seeds are cousins of the GRAIN that farmers *sow* into big fields. Slender grass blades grow tall and bloom. Pollinated by winds, tiny blossoms ripen into clusters of golden grain. Giant machines harvest the grain, separating the seeds from the stalk and the *chaff*. At the mill, grain is ground into flour.

From wheat, oats, rye, barley, and corn come crusty breads, pastries, cereals, and pastas. Farm animals also eat grain. The grain, which is also the seed, is replanted, and the cycle begins anew.

 What food grows standing in water?

Grains

RICE is eaten daily by millions of people around the world.

Like wheat and corn, the rice plant is also a grass. It grows wild in swamps. Farmed rice is planted in paddies, which are fields that have been flooded with water. The young seedlings can reach six feet in height. When the clusters of rice seeds are ripe, the water is drained from the fields for easy harvest.

Brown rice is more nutritious than polished white rice. Flavorful black wild rice is a delicacy.

 What sweet food is made by insects?

Sugars

Bees produce HONEY in the summer for their winter food.

As bees collect sweet *nectar* from the flowers, pollen sticks to their hairy legs. Back at their *hives*, the pollen is used as food. Nectar is stored inside the wax cells of the *comb*, where it turns into honey. In early fall, beekeepers wearing veiled hats to protect themselves from bee stings, remove some honeycomb frames from the hives.

In the honey house, machines spin the combs to draw out honey. The empty beeswax comb is melted into golden candles.

What food is needed for all forms of life?

WATER is *the* most important food. Neither people, plants, nor animals can live without it. Drinking lots of water is healthy. Our bodies are made mostly of water!

Rainwater from clouds helps trees and plants grow. It also provides the drinking water for *springs* and *wells*, and for *reservoirs* that supply water to large cities. Water is naturally recycled when the heat of the sun evaporates it and turns it back into clouds.

Clean water is precious. We must not pollute or waste it.

From Flower to Fruit

The flower is the part of a plant that produces fruit. But to make the fruit, a flower must be pollinated. This is how pollination happens: In the flower's center is the ovary. Above the ovary is the pistil with the stigma at the end. The pistil is surrounded by pollen-covered anthers. Invited by a flower's scent, an insect comes to drink the nectar. Its legs and body get dusted with the flower's pollen. As the insect moves from flower to flower, pollen is brushed against the stigmas. (Some flowers are pollinated by the wind, which blows pollen onto the stigmas.) From the stigma, the pollen travels down the pistil and fertilizes the ovules, turning them into tiny seeds in the ovary. Now the ovary, with the fertilized seeds inside, can grow into a fruit. As the small fruit grows, the flower shrivels and falls off. The seed for the new plant is hidden within the fruit's center.

STIGMA

PISTIL

ANTHER

OVARY

OVULES

Glossary

Aggregate: A cluster or group that forms a whole.

Carbohydrates: Nutrients from plants that supply us with sugars, starches, and fiber.

Chaff: Inedible pieces of stem or husk that are separated from the grain by threshing.

Chlorophyll: A substance in plants that captures the sun's energy and makes the plants green.

Cold-blooded: An animal whose body temperature changes with the air or water temperature that surrounds it.

Comb or *honeycomb:* A structure made of six-sided wax cells built by honeybees in their hives. Bees raise their young and store honey inside these cells.

Crop: A group of plants or animals grown for harvesting.

Dairy: A building or room where milk is stored. It is equipped to manufacture cheese, butter, and other dairy products.

Fungus: Plant life that lacks chlorophyll. Some fungi obtain food from rotting organic matter; others are parasites. Parasites are plants or animals that live off other living organisms.

Gill: An organ used by fish and other water-breathing animals to obtain oxygen from the water.

Hive: A bee house built by a bee colony or a beekeeper.

Homogenize: A process that keeps cream from separating from milk and rising to the top.

Husk: The outer covering of a seed.

Nectar: The sweet liquid that is produced in the center of a flower and collected by bees to make honey.

Nourish: The process of using nutrition and energy to promote growth and sustain life.

Pasteurize: A method of making milk safe to drink by heating it to kill bacteria.

Plankton: Tiny plants and animals that float or drift in water.

Pod: A shell or fruit of a plant that contains seeds.

Pollen: A flower's dust-like spores needed in the process of turning a flower into fruit.

Reservoir: A natural or artificial lake or pond where water is collected for home and industrial use.

Root: The underground part of a plant that supports the plant and draws and stores food and water.

Roughage: High fiber food. The coarse, indigestible parts of food like bran, hay, or fruit and vegetable pulps and skins.

Seed: The part of the plant from which new plants grow.

Sow: To plant seeds.

Spore: A minute reproductive cell of a non-flowering plant such as fungus, moss, or fern.

Spring: Water from underground that pushes to the surface.

Stalk: The stem of a plant.

Udder: The bag-like organ with glands that secrete milk from which a young animal drinks and from which farmers get milk.

Vine: A plant whose stem is too slender to hold itself up. It supports itself by climbing on a sturdier plant, a pole, or a wall.

Well: A hole dug or drilled to get access to an underground, spring-fed pool of water.

Food Guide Pyramid

A GUIDE TO DAILY FOOD CHOICES

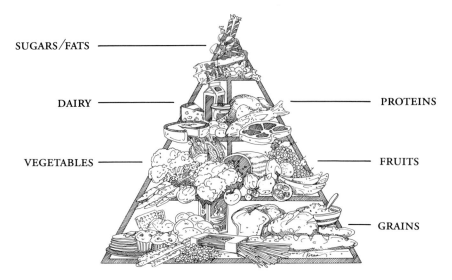

SUGARS/FATS

DAIRY — PROTEINS

VEGETABLES — FRUITS

GRAINS

We can be strong and healthy if we eat a variety of foods each day from all the food groups shown in the pyramid above. The biggest number of servings should be from the grain group on the bottom. As the pyramid gets smaller toward the top, so should the number of servings we eat from those groups.

Our bodies have many parts with different nutritional needs. Skin, bones, inner organs, blood, and muscles function well when they get nutrition from the following foods:

Fruits/Vegetables

FRUITS CONTAIN: vitamins, *carbohydrates*, minerals, fiber.

Fruits are good sources of many vitamins. Vitamins are minute substances that perform important tasks, so that the many parts of our bodies function well. Fruits are also rich in fructose, which is a source of carbohydrates that provides our bodies with energy. Eating fruit quenches our thirst because of its high water content.

FRUIT CHOICES: apple, pear, plum, peach, apricot, cherry, grape, orange, tangerine, lemon, lime, nectarine, pineapple, grapefruit, banana, mango, papaya, kiwi, cactus fruit, melon, quince, date, strawberry, currant, raspberry, blackberry, gooseberry, loganberry, blueberry.

VEGETABLES CONTAIN: vitamins, fiber, minerals, carbohydrates.

Vegetables are healthy foods naturally low in fat and high in fiber. Fiber is indigestible roughage that our bodies need to clean out solid wastes. Vegetables have many essential minerals and vitamins.

VEGETABLE CHOICES (vegetable leaves): spinach, cabbage, Brussels sprouts, kale, chard, parsley, lettuce, mustard, collard, beet and turnip greens, arugula, dandelion, Chinese cabbage, wheat grass; (vegetable stalks): celery, asparagus, rhubarb, kohlrabi, fennel, chive; (vegetable flowers): cauliflower, broccoli, artichoke; (vegetable fruit): tomato, cucumber, summer and winter squash, eggplant, pepper, bean, pea, okra, pumpkin; (vegetable root): carrot, parsnip, turnip, rutabaga, beets, radish, celeriac, burdock, Jerusalem artichoke, potato, sweet potato, yam, peanut; (vegetable bulbs): onion, garlic, scallion.

Dairy

DAIRY CONTAINS: complete protein, minerals, vitamins, fat.

Milk and milk products are rich in calcium, a mineral that is essential for strong bones and teeth. Minerals are natural nutrients that many cells in our bodies need to function properly. Milk products are excellent sources of complete protein.

DAIRY CHOICES: milk, cheeses, yogurt, cottage cheese, cream cheese, buttermilk.

Proteins

MEATS CONTAIN: complete protein, fat, minerals, vitamins.

Meat, like milk, is a source of complete protein, which our bodies need to build, replace, and repair cells and tissue. It also has saturated fat.

MEAT CHOICES: beef, pork, veal, lamb, goat, rabbit, chicken, turkey, duck, goose, pheasant, venison.

FISH CONTAINS: complete protein, fat, minerals, vitamins.

Fish, with few exceptions, are low-fat, complete-protein foods with valuable minerals and vitamins.
SEAFOOD CHOICES: cod, pollack, bass, monkfish, snapper, sole, shad, flounder, sardine, herring, tuna, whitefish, porgy, trout, catfish, shark, salmon; crab, lobster, oyster, mussel, clam, scallop, shrimp.

EGGS CONTAIN: complete protein, fat, minerals, vitamins.

Eggs, like meat and milk, are nutritious because they supply us with complete protein, minerals, and some animal fat. Proteins keep our hair and nails strong and healthy.
EGG CHOICES: chicken, turkey, goose, duck, pheasant, and quail eggs.

LEGUMES CONTAIN: incomplete protein, carbohydrates, fiber, minerals, vitamins, fat.

With the exception of soybeans, legume proteins are incomplete proteins. For this reason, legumes should be eaten together with grains, nuts, seeds, or dairy to complete the protein. Except for oil-rich peanuts and soybeans, legumes are naturally low in fat, but rich in fiber.
LEGUME CHOICES (beans): kidney, pinto, sailor, black, black-eyed, white, red, adzuki, mung, lima, soybean; (peas): green, yellow, chick-peas; also peanut and lentil.

NUTS AND SEEDS CONTAIN: incomplete protein, fat, fiber, minerals, vitamins.

Very rich in unsaturated fats, nuts and seeds are an almost complete-protein food, with many different minerals, some important vitamins, and plenty of fiber.
NUT AND SEED CHOICES: pecan, walnut, hazelnut, almond, cashew, pistachio, Brazil, pine, macadamia; sunflower, sesame, squash, pumpkin, flax.

Grains

GRAINS CONTAIN: carbohydrates, incomplete protein, minerals, vitamins, fat.

Grains are an important fuel and energy food. They supply our bodies with plenty of carbohydrates. Carbohydrates make our muscles function smoothly. Whole grains, with the bran and germ not removed in processing, are important sources of B vitamins and contain a great number of minerals and fiber.
GRAIN CHOICES: rice, wheat, barley, rye, oat, corn, millet, kasha, quinoa.

Sugars/Fats

SUGARS CONTAIN: simple carbohydrates.

Sugars have lots of calories, but practically no vitamins, minerals, or other valuable nutrients. They contain, therefore, what is known as "empty calories." When sugar is eaten alone or in large amounts, it goes directly into the bloodstream, giving a quick burst of energy. Once this energy is burned up, a craving for more sugar can set in. Excess sugar consumption can cause weight gain and tooth decay. Honey, fructose, or maple syrup are considered natural sugars. Beet and cane sugar are refined sugars.
SUGAR CHOICES: cane and beet sugar, honey, molasses, corn syrup, maple syrup, barley malt, fructose.

SATURATED FATS CONTAIN: fat, vitamins, minerals.

Saturated fat is mostly found in animal products and in some tropical plant oils. It usually hardens at a low room temperature. Fat is a nutrient that is needed daily for fuel, energy, growth, and health. However, too much saturated fat in the diet can contribute to weight gain. It can also clog arteries in our bodies and cause heart disease.
SATURATED FAT CHOICES: butter, cream, lard, coconut oil, and palm oil.

UNSATURATED FATS CONTAIN: fat, vitamins, minerals.

Fats from plants, best known as oils, are good sources of unsaturated fats that we need for healthy skin and nervous systems.
UNSATURATED FAT CHOICES: olive, corn, sunflower, safflower, canola, grape seed, avocado, flax seed, wheat germ, walnut, almond, peanut, sesame, and cod liver oils.

Good Nutrition: What Parents Can Do

The mental and physical well-being of children is affected by the foods they eat. A balanced, wholesome diet assures an alert mind, a healthy body, and normal growth.

Unfortunately, numerous children from all population segments are eating unbalanced diets that lack basic nutrients.

The food industry, with aggressive advertising and easy availability, has lured adults and children into buying products of low nutritional value. Highly refined grains and sugars are the cheapest sources of energy generally available. Through processing, they have been stripped of most of the nutrients with which they are naturally endowed.

Children who, over prolonged periods of times, do not eat from all the food groups, may become malnourished. Malnourished children become easily fatigued, are unable to perform well in school, and may be less resistant to sickness. They can be too thin or too fat. High sugar consumption can promote tooth decay and appears to cause hyperactivity.

Here are a few things parents can do for their children's well-being and health:

GETTING FOOD:
• Take children shopping. Bring a shopping list and reuse bags for the groceries.
• Show your children how to read food labels.
• Let them know how to do comparison shopping, based on food quality.
• Teach your children how to grow vegetables and herbs in your garden or in a window box.

COOKING FOOD:
• The kitchen is the heart of the house and should be cheerful, clean, and safe for children.
• Encourage your children to plan menus and help with cooking and baking. It may take some patience when they make a mess at the beginning.
• Serve a wide variety of foods from all food groups. Try new recipes, be creative!
• Be resourceful when it comes to serving healthy food to children. If they don't like cooked vegetables, consider stir-frying, or give them the option to eat them raw, or to drink vegetable juices.

• Be creative in order to encourage a child to eat from all the food groups, like offering a tasty fruit-milk shake to a youngster who is not a big fruit eater.
• Make sure your kids eat a balanced diet. Limit candies, cookies, chips, and sodas. They are too salty or too sugary, low in nutrition, and are frequently loaded with fats. They satisfy the hunger and therefore undermine the body's need for nutrition-rich foods.
• Whenever possible choose chicken, turkey, and fish over red meats.
• If your child decides to become a vegetarian, then you and your child *must* understand how to create meat substitutes. *Diet for a Small Planet*, by Frances Moore Lappe (Ballantine Books), clearly explains the principals for a safe vegetarian diet.
• Serve low-fat milk products.
• Bake and cook using unrefined ingredients, like unbleached or whole-grain flour.
• Make your own cereals.
• Stay away from sugar as much as possible.
• Pack your child's lunch box with nutritious foods. Opt for fresh fruit rather than sugary treats. The teacher will thank you!
• Do not withhold food for punishment or use it as a reward.

THE FAMILY MEAL:
• Show your children how to set an attractive table.
• Share a daily meal at the table as a family.
• Keep meal times pleasurable. This should not be a time for scolding.
• Serve food that looks good. Children, like adults, "eat with their eyes."
• Fill your child's plate according to his or her appetite.
• Good table manners are important.
• End the meal with a compliment and a "thank you" for the cook; and have everyone chip in with the cleanup!

Preparing, sharing, and enjoying wholesome, homemade foods with family and friends is an important part of life.

Celebrating special holidays with traditional meals are important rituals to many people. Therefore, cooking the family recipes should be taught and passed on to the next generation, so that they may keep these traditions alive.